RACISM

© Aladdin Books 1991

Design: Andy Wilkinson
Editorial: Catherine Bradley, Elise Bradbury
Picture Research: Emma Krikler
Illustrator: Ron Hayward Associates

First published in the United States in 1991 by
Gloucester Press, 387 Park Avenue South, New York, NY 10016

Printed in Belgium   All rights reserved

Library of Congress Cataloging-in-Publication Data

Grunsell, Angela.
    Racism / Angela Grunsell.
       p.   cm. -- (Let's talk about)
    Includes index.
    Summary: Discusses the issue of racism and explains how readers can take an informed stand against the myths of racial superiority.
    ISBN 0-531-17279-1
    1. Racism--Juvenile literature. [1. Racism.] I. Title. II. Title: Let's talk about racism.
HT 1521. G78   1991
305.8--dc20   90-43994   CIP   AC

"LET'S TALK ABOUT"

RACISM

ANGELA GRUNSELL

Gloucester Press
London · New York · Toronto · Sydney

Everyone has a right to
respect and justice.
Racism means that
some people get neither.

4

"Why talk about racism?"

Racist jokes, name-calling and violent racist attacks happen all the time. Yet many people try to pretend that racism is not a problem. If you look and listen carefully, you will come across racism every day. Racism means that some people make judgments about you without bothering to find out what you are like. Some people get treated unfairly because of racism. Racism deepens misunderstanding between groups of people who could learn from each other and live together. Thousands of racist attacks take place every year. Many families live in fear because of threats to them and their homes.

This book looks at what racism is, what its effects are and why it is so harmful. It shows how racism comes out in the way people talk. It describes how racism is used by rulers to increase their power and make ordinary people fear each other.

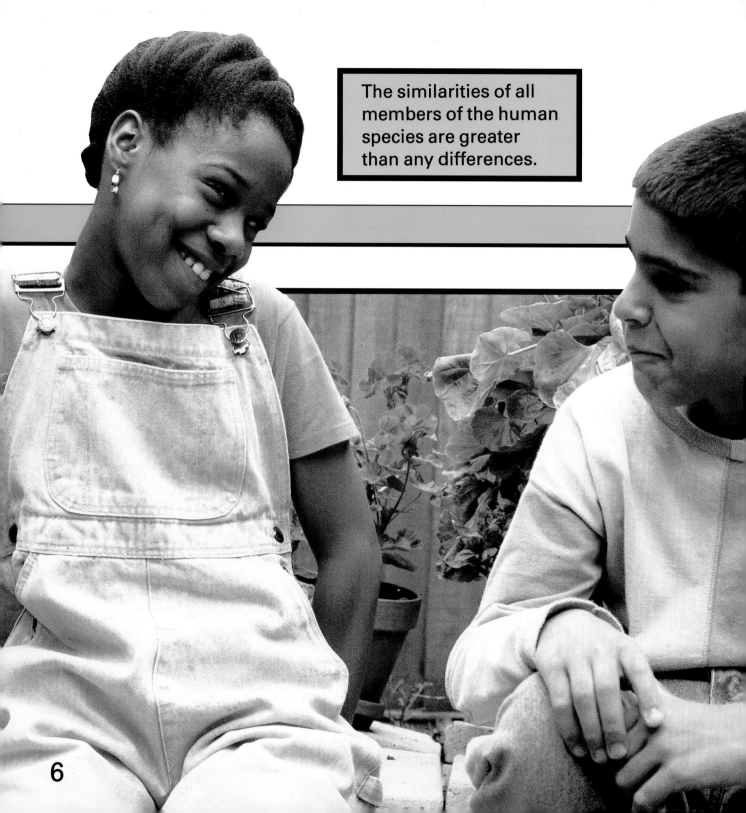

The similarities of all members of the human species are greater than any differences.

"What is racism?"

We all belong to one species, the human species. In order to study the human species, scientists have divided us into groups, or races. Some of us have white skin, some of us have dark skin. Some of us have curly hair, some of us have straight hair. But we are all part of the same species.

Racism is the mistaken belief by some people that their group, or race, is better than others. They think that other groups are "different." But the truth is that everyone is different.

We are all special. You are not the same as your mother or father, brothers or sisters, although you may look like them. There is only one person in the world like you. You may look more like some people in your class than others, but that does not mean you are just like them. Your best friend may speak another language at home and not look like you at all.

Racism occurs when you close yourself off from some people because they come from a different place or kind of people. You decide that they do not belong to your group. You might do this because of the way they look or perhaps even the way they talk.

As a result of racism some groups in our society have more privileges than others. Racial discrimination – which means giving houses, jobs or educational opportunities on the grounds of race – is against the law. But racial abuse happens in many places: on the bus, in the playground, and even in the classroom. Although people can take cases of racial abuse to court, it can be very difficult to prove exactly what happened. However, when someone wins a case of racial discrimination, it shows that people are willing to work for a fairer society.

It takes courage to find out what a person is really like if friends or parents are telling you not to. Michael and Jamal are in the same class. Michael said, "I don't play with blacks." This is racism. The two boys support the same football team, like the same music, share the same favorite foods. If Michael had asked Jamal about himself, he would have found this out. They have more in common than Michael and his cousin. But Michael was prejudiced against Jamal without even speaking to him.

Everyone would think it unfair and silly if only those children wearing the same color clothes were allowed to play together in the playground.

"What is prejudice?"

Prejudice means deciding in advance what someone is like instead of finding out for yourself. Prejudice comes from fear and suspicion. Some people are prejudiced against those of another race. They think that because a person looks or sounds different, that person is not as good as they are.

They will sometimes say "they're all lazy or stupid" or "you can't trust them." If they do form a friendship with someone who belongs to a group they are prejudiced against, they say, "Well she's different." But they do not allow their experience to change their false or stereotyped views about people in that group.

Many people enjoy being supporters of a team without needing to bully or insult the fans of the other team.

"What is a stereotype?"

A stereotype is a fixed idea about what people are like. For example, advertizing uses stereotypes by creating images of "perfect mothers" to sell detergent. If you get stereotyped by others it can be hard to try out different ways of behaving. You may not be treated seriously if you are known as the class clown. Stereotyping reduces whole groups of people to one characteristic, for example, calling all overweight people "jolly." Racial stereotyping means that some teachers expect all black children to be athletic. Stereotypes are bad because they can limit how you see others and how you see yourself.

> Mae Jamieson is a U.S. astronaut. All children need to be able to see that if they want to become an astronaut, a scientist or a judge, it is possible for them to do it.

"Where did racism begin?"

Over the last 500 years European countries invaded the Americas, Africa and Asia. They seized many territories and created countries which they ruled as colonies.

Black Africans were brought to America and sold to rich white farmers to plant and harvest the crops. The black Africans not only lost their freedom, but their families were also torn apart and separated.

It took many years and a terrible civil war for them to regain their freedom. But today many people who have black skin must still fight the racism that came about so long ago.

This map shows how some countries had by 1914 taken over other lands. Today these lands are independent, but they must still struggle for equality.

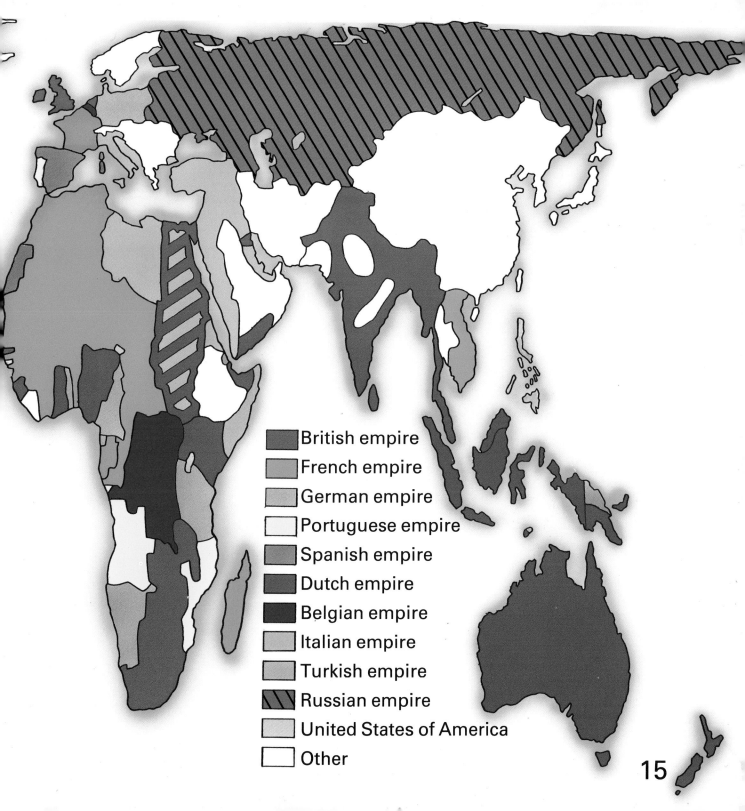

British empire
French empire
German empire
Portuguese empire
Spanish empire
Dutch empire
Belgian empire
Italian empire
Turkish empire
Russian empire
United States of America
Other

15

"How do racist ideas get passed on?"

Very young children are not racist. They trust and accept anyone who is loving toward them. You are not born with attitudes and prejudices. They are taught and learned. Racist ideas get passed on when people talk to others or write or draw pictures. Parents teach children the names to give things. They also teach their own attitudes to them along with the names. A project and an apartment building are both made of the same materials. Yet despite this you might think of them very differently.

Pictures can pass on racist ideas by not showing us people in other places as individuals. Instead, people are often shown as part of an anonymous workforce.

"Why is there racism today?"

Some people today think that they will benefit from being racist. They may be afraid or jealous of other groups. They may blame difficulties in their own lives on other people. They may have learned from their parents to resent and mistrust people from other groups. They may believe the racist stereotypes and ideas that have been passed on to them. They may be white or black, red or yellow. Anybody can be racist. Bullies often use racial differences as an excuse for violent behavior.

This boy is an Aborigine living in Australia. He experiences racism today because his people are denied many rights. In the past European settlers took Aborigine land away by force.

Nazi Germany claimed that Jewish people were an inferior race. Millions of Jews were killed. These Jewish women and children are waiting to go to a concentration camp.

"Why is racism so harmful?"

Racism creates mistrust between people. In some countries, leaders have used resentments between groups to create hatred and suspicion between people. Politicians have used ordinary people's prejudice to get support for their racist ideas and actions.

In the 1930s Hitler and the Nazis in Germany persuaded their followers to blame everything that was wrong in their lives on the Jews. Nazi gangs attacked Jews and destroyed their property. Laws were passed to stop Jewish people from owning their own businesses. The laws also prevented them from having the same rights to health care, education and even protection by the police, as other people. Many Jews fled from Germany to escape from such harsh laws, but some fought back. Others were sent to concentration camps and nearly six million of them died. The Nazis were defeated by other countries in 1945.

The freeing of black leader Nelson Mandela, was brought about by people all over the world who believe that racism and Apartheid are unjust and destructive. He had spent 27 years in prison.

Accepting racist beliefs means hoping that you will benefit from the unjust treatment of other people. Racism means that people are divided against each other instead of learning to live together peacefully.

In South Africa, people of European origin are still holding onto land they have taken over the last 300 years. There are only 4.5 million whites and 22.3 million blacks. Whites own 87 percent of the best land while the blacks have only 13 percent. In South Africa the whites have forced black people to accept an Apartheid (separateness) system. The Apartheid system of laws means that the whites control where black people live and work and even who they can marry. Black children do not get as much money spent on their education as do white children.

These laws have kept wealth and power in the hands of white people. Apartheid is based on racist ideas that black and white are different and should live and develop separately because whites are superior. Black South Africans have never given up the hope of getting their land back. They fight for their rights as human beings. Things are changing because millions of black and white people, inside and outside South Africa, believe that Apartheid is evil and wrong, and should be changed.

"What about racism in our school?"

When you realize what racism can lead to, you can understand that racist incidents are more than just a problem between two or three people. You can begin to see how, in some extreme cases, it can bring about hatred, murder and war. Racism means that people from some groups are attacked in their homes and on the street. They may feel as if nowhere is safe for them. You may want to do something to make your school a safe place for everyone. If you have ever been called racist names yourself, you know how hurtful it can be.

In many schools, children and adults work to stop racism. This painting was done by children who worked together on a charter for human rights after studying South Africa.

Changing how things are can start with individuals getting together with others who are against racism. You have the power to challenge racism in your classroom and your school by talking about it with your teacher.

Your teacher may not know what is happening in the playground or the bathrooms or even in the lunch line until you tell her or him. You and your friends can also talk to your principle about the problem of racism. You may need to get help from parents or other adults. When you have class discussions about racism you will begin to find out what is happening to other children and how they feel about the way in which they are being treated.

Racism is a very complex subject, which goes back a long way in history and is rooted in our language. It is for this reason that everyone must learn about and understand the problems it causes. One way of changing attitudes is to find out more about how other people live. You can add to your enjoyment of life by finding out about things like the languages, religions, food, art and music of groups that you are not very familiar with. You will meet people who at first sight are not exactly like you. You can use this opportunity to ask them about their lives and talk about your own way of life.

The more you know about other people and they know about you, the less you will be divided by racism. The Chinese New Year is celebrated in many countries.

"How do I deal with racist insults?"

Any group can become the target of racism. Feeling good about who you are cannot prevent other people from insulting you, but it can help you to deal with it better. You can learn to avoid some confrontations, by acting with dignity and refusing to let other people annoy you. You may need to judge quite carefully the right moment to stand up for yourself and others, and when to get help, or simply leave a situation quickly. Everyone needs to learn ways of surviving. When people get together to take action against unfair treatment, they can change things.

> You do not have to put up with racial discrimination or bullying. If you need help, ask for it and work out the best way of challenging the people who are upsetting you.

"What can I do?"

This book has shown you how racism works both between individuals and in countries. You have learned that prejudice and stereotypes – even through jokes and comments – create and maintain racist ideas. You will never learn to understand yourself or other people if you let yourself be guided by such ideas.

Although the book has talked a lot about black and white, there are many other examples of racism past and present that you can find out more about.

You can, in ways that work for you, choose to challenge racism when you come across it. You can try to be fair to everyone you meet and to find out more about what they are really like by listening and talking.

Addresses for further information

Martin Luther King Center
for Nonviolent Social Change
449 Auburn Avenue
NE Atlanta, Georgia 30312

American Civil Liberties Union
132 West 43 Street
New York,
New York 10036

What the words mean

Apartheid is the South African system for keeping groups or races apart and enforcing this with laws.

concentration camp is a prison where people are forced to live and work in very poor conditions.

discrimination occurs when people put others at a disadvantage.

prejudice is having an opinion or deciding about something or someone without finding out for yourself – you prejudge.

racism is a belief held by some people that their group, or race, is better than others.

species is a class of living things that are very similar. All human beings belong to the same species.

stereotype is a false picture that links people from particular groups with certain, usually negative, characteristics.

Index

Photographic Credits:
Cover and pages 4-5, 6-7, 8-9 and 28-29: Marie-Helene Bradley; page 11: Topham Photo Library; page 12: Frank Spooner Pictures; page 16: Rex Features; page 18-19: ICI Corporate Slide Bank; page 20-21: The Institute of Contemporary History and Weiner Library; page 22-23: International Defence and Aid Fund for Southern Africa; page 24-25: taken at Dulwich Hamlets Primary School (by Art and Development Education Project); page 26-27: Network Photographers.

PRINTED IN BELGIUM BY
proost
INTERNATIONAL BOOK PRODUCTION